Sweet Juice and Ruby-Bitter Seed

Sweet Juice and Ruby-Bitter Seed

Poems by

Merryn Rutledge

© 2023 Merryn Rutledge. All rights reserved.
This material may not be reproduced in any form, published,
reprinted, recorded, performed, broadcast,
rewritten or redistributed without
the explicit permission of Merryn Rutledge.
All such actions are strictly prohibited by law.

Cover design by Shay Culligan
Cover photo by Margarita Zueva, www.Unsplash.com
Interior illustration by Adrienne Dent, www.adrienneallyndent.com
Instagram: AdrienneDentStudio
Editing by Brett Warren

ISBN: 978-1-63980-332-3

Kelsay Books
502 South 1040 East, A-119
American Fork, Utah 84003
Kelsaybooks.com

*In gratitude for my parents,
Lloyd L. Rutledge
and
Lorene F. Rutledge*

Acknowledgements

Grateful acknowledgements to the editors of publications where poems have appeared, sometimes in earlier versions or with different titles:

As Above So Below: "Changing My Mind," "First Fireflies"

Aurorean: "Passagère"

Avocet: "Worry"

Borrowed Solace: "Natural Occurrences"

Cutthroat: "Deluge"

Feral Journal of Poetry and Art: "A Northerner Faces East"

Mass Poetry, The Hard Work of Hope series: "Mad Libs"

Mocking Owl Roost: "Sightings"

Muddy River Review: "Fox"

Multiplicity: "Serendipity"

Of Rust and Glass: "Room, Patterned in August"

Open Door Magazine: "Jonathan"

Paddler Press: "September Night"

Pensive: "Legacy"

Persimmon Tree: "Appearances"

The Poet: "Full Circle," "Reconsider"

The Poet, The Family Anthology: "Broken"

The Poetry Porch: "At the Shore after Long Absence," "Influenza, October 1918," "Red-Wing Blackbirds Return," "Seeing at Night"

Pudding Magazine: "Belonging"

Pure Slush, Life Span Anthology Series, Marriage: "Speakers"

Snapdragon: "Metamorphic"

Speckled Trout Review: "Safe"

Young Ravens Literary Review: "Eve Celebrant"

Contents

Part I

At the Shore after Long Absence	1
Metamorphic	2
Listening Stone	3
Mountaintop Experience	4
Rumination	6
Sightings	7
Ode to the White Pines Who Are My Neighbors	8
Deluge	10
Worry	12
Seeing at Night	13
Rain	14
Serendipity	15
Staying Put in a Northern Winter	16
Passagère	17

Part II

Summer Solstice	37
A Northerner Faces East	22
Speakers	23
Living Room	25
Natural Occurrences	26
Relief	27
Red-Wing Blackbirds Return	28
Tuning	29
Room, Patterned in August	30
September Night	32
Moving through a Particular Grief	33
The Meaning of Things	34
Fox	35
Walking Past	36
Jonathan	37
Full Circle	39

Part III

First Fireflies	59
Belonging	44
Carnal Desire	45
Safe	47
Mad Libs	48
Noisy Memory	49
Influenza, October 1918	50
Broken	51
Threshold, 1966	53
Summer Luck	54
Bad Boys	55
Legacy	56
Reward	58
Reconsider	60
Cultivation	62
Appearances	64
Eve Celebrant	65
Changing My Mind	66
My First Mango, New Orleans French Quarter	67
Dance Lessons	68

The soul in paraphrase, heart in pilgrimage . . .

—George Herbert, *Prayer*

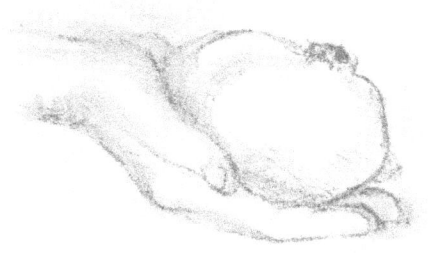

Part I

At the Shore after Long Absence

For John O'Donohue

I crest the dune to behold an ageless majesty unfold—
the elemental conversation of wind and water
revealing to the cliffs and beached boulders
their gradual transfiguration
into grains of granite, pearls of amber quartz,
calcified fragments of ancient life,
and slivers of glittering mica
refined to a ribbon of sky-reflecting sand
that soothes my feet and coaxes my mind
to yield its busy whirr
to the simple sense of a sapphire sea
winking at the sun beyond a lace fringe of waves
that make a rhythmical *clap, clap, clap, clap*
with their other hand, the beach.

Metamorphic

After Anne Carson

Lying awake, night thoughts
blooming like slime mold—

a minute to midnight,
children choke on smoke or drown.

Chaos, everybody dead
after not paying attention

to fire, storms, starvation, migration, wars
elsewhere, until they happen here.

I get up, turn on a light, pick up the stone
she gave me with a note that said *rechargeable*.

Lopsided egg, smooth as skin,
translucent as a newborn's skull.

On one face, a pock the size of a freckle.
On another, a crevice with a cloud inside.

Cool waning or waxing moon, gray-white,
gray-green, marble with cream.

Veins and capillaries run here and there,
rivers viewed from outer space.

The fissures may cleave someday, leaving
jagged edges to be polished by wind and sand.

Under the kitchen bulb, crystal adularescence,
star specks glimmering in a white sky, eye.

Listening Stone

Encountering Joseph Wheelwright's "Listening Stone"
in deCordova Sculpture Park

One cheek of a giant head rests
on the ground where the sculptor found
a boulder that would listen to his dream
The ear tilted skyward hears me come
to imagine the other ear to the ground sounding
worms digging
an upwelling spring
raspy car tires on nearby asphalt
Boulder listened to its forming
in the sagging belly of a glacier
that moved over the face of the earth
now a plinth for Atlas
freed

Mountaintop Experience

We took the slow route, zigzagging
upward to the Continental Divide,

a disappointing apex, bare and colorless to two Easterners
used to the varied green of trees that ribbon our slopes.

We stopped to stretch and walk about.
Pallid sky. Thin air. The massive, bald, stone pate we stood on.

Signs met us. *Fragile ecosystem. Stay on marked paths.
Leave no trace.* Was it this triple caution

that caused us to look again?
Lichen—ruffled silver, ocherous, olive-green.

Splashes of yellow, coral, lavender, lapis.
Tiny flowers clinging to stone or on short stems

seeped, it seemed, from giant granite slabs, wind-smoothed,
overlapping like glacier ice and like a glacier falling

out of sight from—what cliffs or slides? Considering
the awful possibilities made us airplane our arms

like two acrophobic novices who cross a chasm on ropes.
Our eyes sought hoped-for safety in some goal—

except we had nowhere to get to.
Epiphany of flowers. Revelation of stone shifting in time.

Snort of a truck straining toward the crest foreshadowed
how we would hug switchbacks down and down to the plain

and ordinary time, to trace the names of alpine flowers—
moss campion, buttercup, sorrel, twisted gentian, forget-me-not—

whole worlds in ingenuity of flora,
grandeur only our formless souls can fathom.

Rumination

Robin sits in a circle of sun,
feathers fluffed to make him perfectly round,
his breast the blush of a fuzzy peach.
Peaches.

Once a summer, Grandpa drove us to the orchard,
trees spreading all around,
polka-dotted with ripe fruit and busy with bees,
sugar-hungry as we were.

From the truck bed tucked between the rows,
my cousins and I could reach,
feel a peach's juicy weight, twist it free.
Furry skin and all, we gobbled, nectar dripping down.

Grandpa took his time,
ranging among the trees, grazing.
When he found perfection,
he reached into his faded overalls,
drew out his pocketknife, flicked it open,
and anchoring his thumb to guide the blade,
began a slow spiral,
unspooling one long curlicue of peel.
Taking a bite, he chewed thoughtfully
as he gazed down the line of trees
to where the blue sky landed.

Grandpa might not say a word the whole pilgrimage.
I doubt he would have seen it as a celebration
any more than robin means a praise song
by sitting here soaking up the sun.
But each creates a kind of sacrament
of the immemorial present, now and then.

Sightings

> *Hurt coyote by itself seen last evening in Devon Woods*
> *about 6:30 wondering [sic] around.*
>   —Neighborhood email post

Last evening a neighbor saw a lone coyote.
The writer leaves himself out of it.
What difference does it make—
the coyote was seen. Neighbors in Devon Woods should know.
Who knows what a hurt coyote will do.

Coyote circles
to consider a dark shape on the ground next to it.
When the coyote rounds a tree, sun leaves
and the shape goes away.
The hurt place keeps whining to lick it—
the taste of fresh kill, dripping.
The hurt place cries and cries until coyote knows
she is a self by herself seen
and by herself except for the silent shape
who shambles alongside her.

Overhead, giant oaks stand far apart,
branches, roots, and rhizomes out of touch.
Since the woods that had been Devon Woods were razed,
the old trees wonder
how the others who were spared are getting along
over there, there, and there,
and how they might send warnings about a withering rain
that falls in bud-time from long snakes spread across the grass.
They wonder about the coyote, unsteady wanderer.
She sniffs, looks up at the still two-legged who smells of fear.
She must ignore her stinging paw,
try to run, seek the trees to hide
and save the shape who limps beside her.

Ode to the White Pines Who Are My Neighbors

Again today wind grabs you by the hair
and shakes you
blasts your trunks with bruising body blows
Your seedlings flap their fragile arms

I know   it isn't wind's fault   nor rain
The climate-crazed vortices
Frenetic thrashing hither   thither

When I was a child
(yes   you were young then   too)
on summer nights I lay in a camp cabin
whose walls were window screens
I could listen to breezes whisper to your kind
standing companionably together
a cooling canopy
your fallen needles a soft mat for my bare feet
to pad past the forest fringe
cross the dune
and play all day in the sea's tidal foam
I thought these realms would last   like memory

You   who are my neighbors now
(so near my house   where once a forest stood)
watch me drive in   out   in   out
You are right
foul exhaust isn't the half of it
over time

Roaring mowers   chain saws
rattle your root-veins
your whole sustaining system underground
chronically alarmed

A particularly invasive species   the leaf blower
spine-startles   yes   mine too
Its nasal whine overwhelms your sighs
when the occasional   gentler breeze
brushes your needles
fingers fluttering over harp strings

Grass-purifying chemicals
poison you   the fox licking her kits
meandering turkeys' feet   lungs of deer and doe
and ours   yes   ours too

And yet   because you stand there like
everlastingness
I often forget
to remember you

Deluge

After Dorianne Laux

A sudden downpour draws me to my window
Hissing torrents gush over gutter rims
drown the sidewalk
pool in window wells
Sky-buckets-full spill

        spilled from the well to fill the tubs for the pig slaughter
        back then
        how I dreaded the bucket chain dropping *chaca chaca*
        harbinger of the butcher—my Grandpa—sawing on bone

Now an entrail-ripping rain
crazed-to-crack-foundations rain
slanting   thrashing   when-will-it-end rain
blurs the screens and blinds me
as though the windows were eyes

        mucous-stuck from pinkeye
        when I was a kid trying to read the world

Not much drip   drip   soothing-drip rain anymore
or rain-spout-gurgling-wake-up-to-sparkling-grass rain
or run-barefoot-through-shallow-puddles rain

No   a snare-drum-corps-*ratatat*-to-war rain
Staccato-machine-guns-*rrrrrrrr* rain
abetted by wind that buffets tall pines in the woods nearby
twists trunks willy-nilly with blasts
from north   west   east
then jerks around again

    like the rabid fox that lurched in senseless zigzag
    down my street last summer
    of storms and wildness

Tricksters-in-a-gale-shaking-fists-to-conjure-ruin rain
Spirits-born-from-hubris-cackling-over-cauldrons rain
Oh you earth   wind   and sky
what the choices we have made have made

Worry

unreachable itch
wasps abuzz in a sealed jar
stench from the open graves of certain memories
circuitry of errors, past and possible,
dull, unspecific bone ache

until beneath my window
a winged shadow slides across the grass
disappears beneath a spindly pine
near the top of which a hawk lights
beside a bulging nest where three hatchlings
shriek and stretch their scrawny necks
toward their mother's fresh catch and satisfaction

Seeing at Night

Leaning forward and furrowing her brow,
the sales consultant asked, *Didn't I want room-darkening shades?*
Without waiting for an answer, she pulled from her case
the sample that showed how a charcoal lining shuts out light.
Make my bedroom a vault? I didn't say it but it clarified things.
No, I said as evenly as I could, *I want the white, translucent ones,
the kind I can keep open at the top.*
I didn't tell her but I'm telling you
that along with a little privacy, I want to lie awake
visited by moonlight and strings of words that come like stars,
haunted by moonless black where memories stalk,
nuzzled by winter mornings' slow reveal.
I am telling you this as I sit where I can watch
the slanting sun engrave the sky with stately pines
and imagine the few, quivering leaves
that cling to the mountain ash
are Cedar Waxwings hovering near the cold-fermented berries
they will pluck and drink next spring.

Rain

Catching the gardener's eye as she moved
among the roses snipping faded blooms,
my beloved called, *Just where do you clip
to encourage new buds to come?*
When she smiled, he sang, *What an evening!*
lustily inhaling the musky, after-rain smell
and pointing out to passersby
the petals jeweled with tiny suns.
Before she could answer about the roses,
Martin offered how you could hose a garden,
even, as he once had, pipe water
from a mountain stream—and things will grow,
but lazily and pale, whereas a slow-soaking rain
somehow *engages vitality.*
A crowd began to gather as the gardeners
shared their avocation—the rose tender
stooping down between the bushes to show us
how she coaxed more blossoms to form.
She said a scientist once told her
twenty-seven conditions cohere when it rains.
Just think, she said and Martin did think,
raising his copious eyebrows to show it.
They met in silence then, as though to say
a gardener's work is always awe.

Serendipity

After unsuccessfully Googling my problem—
the milky film on my dishwasher walls—
I was leafing through the Kenmore manual
and poking my head in my appliance
to eyeball what was on the parts list
when the word *filters* caught my eye.

You're supposed to clean the filters—who knew?
I just moved in and reading directions isn't my thing.
Back inside the machine, under the bottom rack
where I didn't think anybody but Kenmore repair
would ever stick their head, I sought to plumb
the mystery of where the filters hid.

I found the handle of a paring knife,
rusty and unmanned by the loss of its blade,
a crusty dime that raised questions
about what the previous homeowners ate,
and sea glass sanded smooth by spinning washer blades
and lodged between two dirty filter screens.

After scrubbing each one with an old toothbrush
I found under the sink, I climbed back on the web,
where I located a product called *Finish*
that promised to remove a mineral film.
I felt hopeful, like when you're nearing the end
of a long board game and you look up to find

the rain that kept you indoors has stopped
so you can go for a walk around the lake,
where mysteries are not for solving—
like how a whirl makes drying leaves pirouette on toe point
and how, just before it slips away, the slanting sun flares
to burnish a stand of yellowing beech to gold.

Staying Put in a Northern Winter

In the dead of winter,
silken filaments crisscross
the inside of my living room skylight.
Glittering tinsel.
Spiders aren't stupid, my husband used to say,
They know how to fix a feast.

In the dead of winter,
brown squirrel,
who moved into the neighborhood last summer,
climbs my window screen.
She stretches her limbs the way rock climbers do,
disappears into a gutter, pops up with bulging cheeks,
and scurries along the roof with springy alacrity.

One silent night,
barred owl perches in the pines outside my bedroom.
He's come each fall since I moved here, close to the woods.
He *hoo-hoo-hoo*s his mate,
haunting stillness with desire.
In the dead of winter.

Email from a friend comes with a selfie attached.
She sits on a Florida beach.
Beats New England in the dead of winter, she opines.

A bottle fly suns on my south-facing window,
gazing at what, I wonder.
Amazing ommatidia making mosaics.
His iridescence glorifies green.

Passagère

Puisque tout passe, faisons la mélodie passagère . . .
Since everything passes, let us make fleeting melody . . .
—Rainer Maria Rilke

Most years, spring here takes its time
as icy earth resolves to mud that lasts for weeks
in what Vermonters call the fifth season,
meaning either boring vernal prologue
or smeary substitution.

This spring there was no in-between
but a quick turn from one day to the next.
I rose expecting bleak monotony
and instead beheld the serviceberry
new born in silken, fawny buds.

In three days' time they burst, petals
trembling, then bowed in a crisp breeze
to leaves pushing in behind.
Discarded petals lay on dormant grass
like a first dusting of autumn snow.

Part II

Summer Solstice

Today is the moment
of the deepest breath
where dread waits

a slack tide
when the swell of summer
suspends the sunset

brief pause
before the current
pulls light back in
the ebb of winter tide

I'm not afraid of being dead
but the turn toward death
is another matter

I've sat close by   waiting
already drained by grief
as life fades

father   then mother
sliding over the brink
with a final exhalation

Evening comes
From now on
the sun subsides
slowly at first

the days will shorten
then quicken
toward immersion in dark
dominion of cold

A Northerner Faces East

For Frank

In winter, wherever I could find
its beams
in houses, hotels, office towers—
like a pilgrim seeking Mecca,
I used to tilt my face
to the slanted sun,
my eyes closed so even eyelids
warmed a little.

As I grow old, I crave
a complement of senses,
face gently drawn toward
the solar rays,
eyes wide to watch shafts
of light stream between pine trunks,
tawny as foxes,
and lines of shadows
penciled on new snow.
My footfalls on the sparkling powder—
brush, brush, hush.
Pause to receive
how our bodies breathe,
these trees and me.

*What millions of breaths have I
not noticed,* my brother whispered
just before his last one.

Speakers

He slumped on the coach across from me,
staring, it seemed, at nothing.

You made me get rid of my Carlson speakers.

Inside me shrilled an alarm
this stranger who resembled
my husband likely didn't hear.

You wanted newer ones, remember?
We had been happy.

You made me, he said.

His head, neck, and hands stained yellow from bile.
We were waiting for it to clear his body
              so he could start chemo.

No chemo.

Instead, a technician in ER glided
her ultrasound wand over his belly.

Splotches on the monitor behind his head—
red, yellow, orange. Flames.

I asked her what the colors meant.
I'm not supposed to say,
she told the monitor.

Martin grunted when the wand kneaded the flesh
              on one spot.
Oh, that kind of infection, he muttered
              to the ceiling.

In my head, I scrolled down
the list of warnings in the notebook
his oncologist had given us.

The patient didn't speak again.

Living Room

> *The house . . . is a "psychic state."*
> —Gaston Bachelard, *The Poetics of Space*

I am sick of patiently tending
      my husband
while he waited   for death
on sofas   staid
at right angles   ladylike
as they held him   on their laps
for a wretched month
of silent agony   until
crying out when pain   reared
he pitched   forward
wracked
                      done

I'm hacking
      couches
tearing limbs
          off chairs
to make
      a pyre
and while the fire
              snaps and hisses
I'm going to
      pry nails
screeching from the walls
claw hinges
            wailing
        with a crowbar
to keen
in space
            the wreck
    inside me

Natural Occurrences

Later I realized that when cold settled in,
the autumn of my distraction, Boxelder beetles
colonized the house while cancer carved lesions in you.
All winter, beetles squirmed through cracks
to lounge around and soil the walls with feces.
In spite of your death, spring came early and strong.
The warming walls extruded beetles that by thousands
coated the foundation and beached on windowpanes.
My counterassault with soapy spray made
clumps of bugs with crippled wings fall away
while legions under them roused to fly into my hair,
down my neck, and finally finding their summer host,
the ash tree you saved after the ice storm broke it,
they stained the bark with blooms of bloody progeny.

Relief

In difficult times carry something beautiful in your heart.
—Blaise Pascal

After a long climb
I reach
the crown atop a bald hill

A lone maple
broader than my outstretched arms
so tall it combs the clouds

Lonely and wind-worn
I lay my cheek
on cool moss clinging to bark
etched like canyon gullies

How old are you
What storms have tried to break you
How do you remain

Thick bare branches
the sinuous trunks of elephants
trumpet skyward

Red-Wing Blackbirds Return

On a steely day in March, my sister and I
breathe hard from heaving snow off my driveway.
June, who lives in the South, grows tired from novel
exertion. I've had more practice, but I'm mortally tired
from carrying the weight of interminable winter and grief.
Overhead a cardinal trims the sky in swooping
scallops, singing *do-whee-to, do-whee-to, do-whee-to*,
momentarily loosening the shroud that wraps my mind
in my husband's dying days, my shrunken life,
and the taunt of daily mail that insists he lives.
How sweet to hear my sister's breath and movement,
for months have passed without anyone here but ghosts.
We pause, leaning on our shovels. A chorus
of voices trills from the woods, the first Red Wings.
Oh, you have them too, June says.
Remember them in Arkansas on Grandpa's farm?
I heave into memory, seeing the July-ripe fields
rippling with heat, but hear no birds when I query
the past. Right now I can barely recall the heart-leap
each year when here in Vermont, Red Wings' return
points me toward a spring that by all other signs
is impossible to believe in. In the coming days,
as June calls on hosts of ancestors whose qualities
and wisdom witness to hope from far-off lines,
my ears slowly awaken to Grandpa's Red Wings
feasting and singing *pthrrreee-pthreeee-pthreee*.
My sister magnifies the incarnate force of birds
who yearly return to the pale North—even now
to the lonely habitat inside me. Hear the company.

Tuning

Stepping into the cool hermitage from where
St. Seiriol set out each day to pray the length of Anglesey,
I sense a resonance of thanks and petitions
by countless fervent folk who called here.
Your rapt face tells me their psalms also sing in you.

Later, when we find speech again, you tell of crossing
other thresholds that pulse with incorporeal prayer.
I know, because my first intimation, long before we met,
rebounds—martyred monks chanting as I walked
among the crumbled columns of a ruined nave.

Such visitations marked our common time—
echo of chants in the charred shell of a Cistercian abbey,
druid incantations still stirring in a circle of cairns,
how St. Francis' and his friends' footfalls imprint
the olive grove beneath Assisi's sun-washed cliff.

I wonder if something left of us, twin witnesses
and maybe also instruments,
will someday sound in souls of travelers.
Near the Tuscan coast, from an abbey emptied by plague,
comes the murmur of monks blessing pilgrims' need.

Room, Patterned in August

A house that has been experienced is not an inert box.
—Gaston Bachelard, *The Poetics of Space*

I startle just before falling
down a dark dream well
but not before sensing
that this, my living room,
is a hollow vault again.
Rivulets of dread find cracks
in the plaster walls
of the as-usual-day-by-day,
which crumbles.
A dear friend moved away today.
My aging sister will soon shrink
into a small retirement-home box,
her last before an urn.
It is late August,
when the slanting sun
points toward shorter days.
Darkness falls fast.
In August I have three times
lain on this couch
too ill to write, read, eat,
my mind furnished in misery.
It was August when I was squeezed
between a wall of grief
after my husband died
and a wall of projected shadows
of thieves who stole all peace
after he was gone.
He fell sick in August.

In this room he lay
listless, jaundiced,
his spirit slack.
By All Saints' Eve,
the whole house
was hollowed out
for woe.

September Night

Awake again,
my heart pulsing with restless grief—
regret, sorrow, the burning cuts
of betrayals by certain ones
whom I thought would offer help.
Darkness shrills with cricket ululation.
There isn't much time to answer longing.

Sliding through the open window,
a breeze brushes my cheek
like another's breath.
Rustles my hair—
a lover's hand.
Let these phantoms suffice.

Moving through a Particular Grief

I
The word *grief* bundles pain into a shape
and labels it a known thing like a shroud or casket.
This spare word barely touches the surface
of a bottomless lake—seizure, paralysis, drowning.
I grieve seems to map a territory,
but I learned all borders are chimerical.

II
When you died, I fell off the edge of the world,
which is flat after all.
Tumbling through space, I reached for handholds—
the blush of sunset, a hawk's arresting screech,
Rumi, Rilke, the frayed ropes of faith.
I called to you. Nothing.

Instead came those who would seek to destroy.
Had I imagined an afterlife, I would have thought
I might regain something of you in memories,
even murmurings soul to soul,
but my woe is absence, rage, and fear that exiles sorrow.

III
The worst happens.
You wasted, rotted, died. No good-bye.
The cruel aftermath blindsides me.

Then how, while flailing in the dark,
can I dream of light?
A stranger tells me I am beautiful.
Sun warms my face.
Feet find the foamy edges of spent waves
that stroke the beach and slough sorrow.
A little.

The Meaning of Things

a leather jacket we bought while strolling through Florence
one custom-fit tuxedo, too big for his final, shrunken form
five faded, threadbare shirts, for tending our small garden
sixty cubic yards of office equipment—
thirty-year-old integrated circuits and motherboards
a set of dowsing rods
College Physics, spotted with mildew
(*The principles remain,* he'd say)
fifty-two linear feet of manuals for obsolete software
four hundred thirty collections of vocal scores—
Mozart masses, *Hugo Wolf, the Complete Songs*
all six hundred Schubert lieder
four crowbars of various lengths
five chain saws, electric and two-stroke gas
thirty-one bank boxes, dated, with content lists—
last century's bookkeeping logs in his first wife's scrawl
a wooden box in a dresser drawer—
one hundred bicentennial quarters
a promissory note paid a half-century ago
three expired passports stamped for travel around the world
his wedding ring, which I had resized to keep him close

Fox

Our fox appeared one last time
the day I sold your things at a yard sale—
fur-lined gloves worn to the shape of your hand,
your mother's recliner where you waited for death,
the oiled chain you kept for a quarter-century
after you used it to rescue a mud-stuck traveler.

Fox crouched on our front stoop and watched me
as I moved among the parts of you I would shed.
Pitifully thin, mangy coat, bare skin scabrous, red.
Your sagging, hairless skin, angry from chemo invasion.
At last fox looked away, got up,
limped toward the woods and marsh beyond.

Have I told you he stopped by the week you died,
when I prowled our suddenly silent house?
Pausing mid-step, forefoot raised,
he held me in a glass-eyed gaze.
For a moment I felt less stranded as I recalled
moonlit winter nights when he crossed the yard,
shadowing the snow phantom-like
while we stood arm in arm admiring
russet coat, floating tail, graceful gait.

Walking Past

The one I remember
sat slumped on the sidewalk
near the entrance to Saks Fifth Avenue
No coat
No hat or gloves
No socks
Old shoes

Right next to the emporium's
wide brass doors
she leaned against the wall
legs akimbo
on pavement so cold
it bit through my boot soles
stung my carefully covered fingers

She asked just once before
we invited the polished doors
to revolve us inside
where we bought my husband
leather gloves
fur-lined
to replace the pair
he had left somewhere

After he died
I sold the almost-new ones
at a yard sale

The woman's parchment face
empty like her upturned palms
I remember thinking
she could die here today

Jonathan

1990–2018

For my sister and brother

After prowling the loveless pen where his birth mother kept him,
he found a wider world in you.

A toddler runs, whole body laughing
except for eyes that wear a startled look from early loss.

Bullied for his brilliance and outbursts of dismembering grief,
he absorbed his peers' assurance of unworthiness

while giving out unguarded love, as when, a small boy, he touched
our mother's cracked cheeks and pined that she would one day die.

Hungry to learn the world by heart,
he hunted fossils, wrote a book when he was nine,

befriended Hell's Angels who crashed a peace march
he was walking with a Buddhist monk,

fed and stroked the wounded animals at the refuge,
even the slit-eyed snakes and armadillos.

Later, in AA, he cupped his ear to his brethren's hard shells
to listen to the ocean roar of their souls' motion.

Now that he is gone, I meet his avatars in young men
in subways, airports, city streets—

the ones who decorate themselves with earrings, chains,
and tattoos patterned like snakeskin.

Once I would have disregarded them as freaks.
Now I know to love them as they are.

If there is such a thing as resurrection, it was your raising Jon,
and though he stumbled into darkness more than once,

you kept a steady gaze on his better selves
until he was ready to grant himself a share of love.

Full Circle

Holding hands, we stand in a circle and sing
the old songs that remind us who we are.
A table worn like the wooden plank at Grandma's
brims with the bounty of a farm that dreams of our forebears—
cucumbers, squash, tomatoes, beans. Sunset.
My father's whispered welcome the evening he died,
Come on in, we'll feed you all,
as though he would rise to sow and harvest again.
Here on a hill above the fertile fields
the dead dwell in us. My sister leans in.
You're safe, say her eyes
to affirm the end of a long ordeal of betrayal
by a woman I left. Peace comes in, folded
into furrows seeded with loss and what remains.

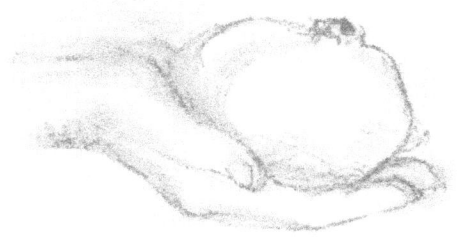

Part III

First Fireflies

Fireflies, come to celebrate desire,
bring me back to summer nights
when we sat on grown-ups' laps
lulled by the to and fro of rocking chairs,
lingering heat, and family voices
lowing like the cows beyond the fence.
In the deepening dark we cousins watch
for insect flash, then rouse and run
into the stardust to catch the magic bugs
in cupped palms now lantern-lit.
Against my skin, a fluttering tickle
like when my mother's feathery
eyelash brushes my kissed cheek.
Opening our hands, we set the tiny beacons free
and spread our arms to wings,
tilting our faces skyward to the bigger lights
that spin around our haloed heads.

Belonging

Mom, my aunts, and Grandma put on flour-sack bonnets
and boots, and carrying pails, galumph toward the garden
two abreast down the tractor tracks.
Heat chases the morning cool, so I wait in the house
until I hear the chain on the well bucket jingle as it drops.
Soon water drums the bottoms of the galvanized tubs
in which the women rinse cucumbers and beans
and dunk potatoes and carrots lumpy with loam.
They draw fresh water to cool down the melons.
The women chat as they scrub, snap, and shell
until the middle of the morning,
when Grandma makes her percolator purr
and we breathe in the earthy coffee smell.
I get a mug like the grown-ups',
only mine comes pale with cream.
After dinner, the men will pitch horseshoes
under the walnut trees where there might be a breeze.
They'll split cool melons with their pocket knives.
We'll stoop over the smiling wedges
as juice runs down our chins, and after,
nobody cares if you wipe your mouth with the back of your hand.
Then a grown-up will say,
I b'lieve these are even sweeter than last year's, Mama and Daddy,
and everybody nods their heads.

Carnal Desire

little girl in a frying sun
sandal soles burned bacon
on a sidewalk
straight as Pixy Stix from Grandma's house
to the Branch General Store
      step
over a crack
don't break your mother's back
tuck your toes
because
snake might be sliding out of the ditch
this side of the
      highway
freight trucks growl and charge
heave hot wind
      dust
your tongue chalky
don't let them knock you down
got to get to town
though not much of one
a row of wooden storefronts
paint long gone and mostly empty
      now
climb three steep steps to the pocked plank porch
tobacco wad spit stained
go to tippy toes to grab the handle of the wheezy screen
blink in the dark cool
      inside
the long, curved face of a glass case
flush with the whole firmament of candy

       Mars bars
            Milky Way
                  Butterfingers
                        Bit-O-Honey
                              Almond Joy
stretch a skinny arm to the man
and let go of a sweaty nickel
peel the crinkly wrapper
strip by strip like a ripe banana
take it slow
        now
back to Grandma's
in tiny bites
smeary lip licks
make it last all the way
        along
with a feeling anything good
can happen under this cloudless sky

Safe

Thunder growls. Out back my father hacks
another weed, looks up, clutches the hoe,
and heads in, passing Mother, who strides to the clothesline
to free the sheets already whipped by wind.

Big sister and brother appear out of nowhere,
their arms full of flashlights and comics, and dragging a rug
to set up camp in the closet at the center of the house.
I'm five and a baby to them, but their look includes me.

Lightning flashes with startling cracks and the hot wind
of a wolf's breath shakes our house made only of wood.
I know an Arkansas storm is bigger than almost anything—
it can snap trees and make any house go blind.

Here in the closet my sister and brother are calming
the dark with their flashlights, their legs tucked up near mine.
Beyond this wall our parents guard the windows
where hail burns like my cheeks do when sparklers spit fire.

Mad Libs

As fall lumbers into winter,
my grandson fills more and more of the blank spaces

in our Mad Lib tales with *hibernating bears.*
In COVID-crazy weekly calls

we two hermits try to claim as comic
the incomparably absurd:

remote first grade—an iPad
where Marcel learns to read *paused* and *poor connection,*

words that appear like flashcards taunting him to say
the maddeningly obvious when his screen goes blurry or blank.

In December, Marcel begins to complain of headaches.
I recall reading that isolated children's bodies hurt.

Excepting some few eremites,
our species only ever lived in caves in groups.

So, brave boy, let rippling laughter answer longing
as we imagine hibernating bears,

not as solitary sleepers, but great balls of fur
filling the dark spaces where hope waits.

Noisy Memory

Grandpa formed a Z as he napped on his side, knees bent,
arms crooked, one palm a pillow, top hand shading his eyes
from us as we fake-tiptoed around him to loudly whisper—
Please Grandma, saltines and Kool-Aid for our house.
As the two oldest cousins, Jake is a dictator dad
like his real one and I'm a bossy mother like mine,
our brothers and sisters the luckless kids who, like Grandma, obey.

The screen door thwacks behind the last one to run
back to our playground, a concrete slab
where henhouses used to rustle and fuss.
Our snake-safe stage suggests our plan—
our kid serfs must heave the coil of chicken wire upright
and unwind the whorl to make a circle house,
which we decide is too bare.

So we race back to the farmhouse,
fling the screen door wide, fly in with the flies,
and forget to whisper our demands—
Towels for beds, Grandma, and Sears catalogs for chairs!
Busy kneading biscuits for dinner for the hordes,
she tucks her chin and clucks,
wipes her hands on her apron, and fetches things.

Grandpa lies an unmoving Z amid the commotion
I wish for now as I lie alone on endless afternoons,
my grandchildren far away as COVID coils to strike.
Maybe Grandpa wasn't napping after all,
but saving the sounds of revels he would trace
through memory's maze, as I do while I wait
for my loved ones to bring back happy havoc.

Influenza, October 1918

First Grandpa took sick, stumbling in from the pasture
as though he'd been snake-bit
and falling into bed where he nearly died.
After the crisis, in the hours between nursing baby Louise,
Grandma went out to wash the bodies of neighbors who died—
until the night she came back to find Louise wheezing,
already blue from lungs that would drown.
Come morning, though the little red head lay still
and Grandma's full breasts must have ached,
she trudged to the barn to milk the Jersey
and dug potatoes that lay like tiny heads in the sucking clay.
Then she washed Louise, put her in her going-to-church dress
and drove with Grandpa the twenty-some miles
to the nearest photographer
so they could always bring their firstborn's face to mind.
She and Grandpa never spoke much that I could see.
Did something between them die that day?
Did they blame each other for bringing death home
or did they blame themselves?
What was it like come spring when Grandma's body swelled
with another child, who would be my mother?

Broken

Upside down on Grandma's playset
trying to swing the trapeze.
I'm a dolphin diving until
my bent legs slip from the bar.
Hammers behind my face
thump   thump   throb.

Old hen upside down in Grandma's grip,
blood gushing from where her head was
before the cleaver slammed down.
The body jerks,
then wings go limp and splay.
Grandma tosses the head
in the slop bucket for the pigs,
rips out clumps of feathers,
reddish brown like Aunt Alma's hair.

Slumped on the doctor's table,
I watch blood   drip   drip   drip
on my sunsuit.
Nose is broke. His tone is flat.
Like raw hamburger in there.

Back at Grandma's, I lie quietly hurting
while she, Mom, and my aunts
tilt the afternoon toward dinner,
when the family tells Grandma
how good the chicken is.
She keeps her *nevermind* face on,
lips clamped the same as when
she drives a fence post,
reaches an arm inside Jersey to pull out a calf,
or raises her hoe
to chop off a snake's head like it was a weed.

By the time I'm helping the women cook—
too big for swing sets
and old enough to understand about breasts—
cancer's gone wild inside Grandma's.
Mom and her sisters don't mean for me to hear—
Where Daddy hit her? Aunt Alma sputters.
Not a question, more like rage let loose—
and suddenly I'm upside down, falling again.
Grandma's *nevermind* face—
what throbbed behind it?

Threshold, 1966

You're sooo screwed up,
I hiss and head for the phone
to tell Sue about my prudish Mom
who thinks I'll catch what Robin got
with a boy in the back seat of his car.

Before Robin leaves for the whole school year,
She, Ellen, Jessie, and me
want to go to the drive-in Friday night
in Sue's parents' Rambler with the front seats
rolled all the way back to make a bed

like a slumber party when we were kids.
Only now we're sixteen so we make fun of a date
with boys we kiss while they knead our breasts
and slide their fingers up our skirt until
we take their hand away or not, if we like them.

Mom says I can't be friends with Robin anymore
and no last "girls' night out" either.
My belly's sick with mad, sad, sorry.
Sure, Robin went too far, but why
tear us apart and make her disappear?

Summer Luck

Like twin chimps grooming a scruffy back,
we combed our weedy suburban lawns
in search of a lucky find.

*I'm looking over a four-leaf clover
that I overlooked before.*
Is that how we knew four leaves made a charm?

What was luck back then, anyway?
Forgotten Lifesavers in the pocket of my shorts?
A penny Susan spied on a sidewalk in town?

Our mothers safe because we didn't
step on a crack, break your mother's back
while jumping hopscotch squares?

Not vaporizing in the mushroom cloud
our school's air raid drills prepared us for?
Better not to dwell on cause and effect.

Enough, the summer days without any obligation.
Following the trail of a meandering tendril.
Biting sour clover for a citrus burst.

Pom-pom blossoms that tickled our palms.
An earthworm glistening like a wet tongue.
Susan's bare, bronze shoulder touching mine.

Bad Boys

I'm convinced that most waywardness is creativity turned backwards.
—Joy Harjo, *Soul Talk, Song Language*

Cousin Daryl told whoppers his daddy called lies. *Snapping turtle big as a tire wheel. Big ole water moccasin thick as my Daddy's arm.* The sting at the end of his father's arm didn't change much about his voluble son. As a grown man, the fish Daryl catches are invariably *huge,* and Montana, where he got rich selling houses, is *the best place to live in the whole US of A.*

My baby brother Kyle started kicking holes in doors when he was three. In school, he didn't sit still, raise his hand, or read. Kyle told me one time after a teacher conference, Mom broke down crying in the parking lot. He watched her shoulders heave but felt he couldn't do anything for her because he really had failed everything but recess. After trying one thing and another, our parents sent him to wildlife camp, where he learned scads of bird species from just hearing their calls. Dr. Kyle still has trouble reading, but he likes listening to his patients. And birdsong.

Then there was Jon, who I made out with in the woods the summer I was thirteen. He was eighteen and smelled like a spilled bottle of English Leather. My parents warned me he was trouble, but we didn't stop until he suddenly disappeared. I wonder if he was bored after graduating high school or maybe just tired of being poor, because he joined the army. They shipped him off to Vietnam before he could find out who he was.

Legacy

1954
When we get to the store, Mom'll give me a nickel
to buy a white sack of malted milk balls,
chocolate going to sweet, white inside.
Little Rock is fun until Mom grips my hand
as Negroes pass and her fear pours into me.

1955
Too much coffee, your knees'll turn dark.
Grandma hands me a cup half-full, pale with cream.
Legs dangling from the grown-up chair
between her and my aunts, I sip in silence
that knows it's a fact and a shame to get stained.

1959
Worse, a dark face, whether brown from farming
or born dark, *colored, nigra,* as dainty relatives say.
Tumbling from the hot car after the two-day drive from D.C.,
I wait my turn to be seen by Grandma, who cups her hands
around my cheeks and clucks, *My, but aren't you brown.*

1964
Heading outside, Grandma nods to the row of bonnets.
I mind her, tying on a floral cotton contraption,
stiff with battens like a prairie-wagon top.
Sun so bright it waters your eyes in heat
that prickles your arms and wiggles the far-off edges of the farm.

1966
Sprawling west from Memphis, rich delta where dark figures bend,
each one dragging a white sack heavy with cotton bolls.
Barefoot kids wait on sagging stoops of weathered shacks.
Convict crews dig in sizzling culverts as cops watch with guns.
Black prisoners with white overseers.

1968
My parents hailed the law in '64 and the one in '65.
We honored King and mourn his loss, but on the yearly trek
to Arkansas, in a tone that tells the cost, Dad says, *You know,
Civil Rights discussions will raise a family fuss.*
I start to speak, then swallow hard.

Reward

Mrs. Sayre snapped at mistakes, stinted praise, strangled joy
as she stood over us smelling sour, a fist on each hip,
sweat stains in each armpit.
When anybody asked *why* about science or a silly rule,
she stretched her lips to a thin, straight line
that made the crooked hair in the mole on her chin
point like a finger.

I mostly kept my head down,
learning what we were supposed to—
the history of Virginia, told as the story of the real America.
I liked wandering into Franklin's experiments, the Adams' farm,
but our textbook lured me back to local lore—
Give me liberty or give me death,
Jefferson claiming *we hold these truths*,
pictures of neat plantations worked by brown blurs,
like Mount Vernon, a few miles from my house.
When somebody asked *why* about the slaves,
Mrs. Sayre's mouth drew a line.

At the school assembly at the close of the year,
while Mrs. Sayre spread manurey breath on our heads,
I heard the principal call my name—
the Daughters of American Revolution History Award—
a red, white, and blue pin in a velvet box.
My stomach felt funny—fluttery proud but tumbly.
Who were these daughters giving me a prize?
Not my ancestors, who were not rich colonial wives
but hardscrabble farmers posing with slaves
in the cracked picture my uncle once showed.
Relatives who still whipped with their filthy tongues?
Faceless slaves in our history book?

I liked marching to the stage,
the pretty pin, and how Mrs. Sayre's tyranny
could not override my earnest essays, perfect tests.
But at the end of the day I put my reward in a drawer
with all the question marks—thin, barbed hooks.

Reconsider

After Steve Scafidi

Remember when Uncle Victor showed us the picture?
The one of our ancestors
back before some of them moved to Arkansas.
Mississippi, was it?
Mother, father, a gaggle of kids posing
in front of an unpainted house—
yeah, clapboard like Grandma's, only even more sorry-looking.
Seemed to me Uncle Victor was pleased to show it around.
Grandma, Aunt Maddy, Dad's brothers, cousins
fanning themselves in the summer heat and trying to piece together
how far back our people up and moved.
In the cracked picture, three slaves off to the side
and just a few heads nod after somebody said, *Lookie there.*
Up until then I always thought
(I say *always,* as if there's such a thing as *always*
when you're a kid and don't think much
about what seem like ancient times)—
always thought we were just Arkansas-poor, country,
and largely cut off way up in the Ozarks.
Now we've lived past Civil Rights,
modern-day lynchings, and Black Lives still don't Matter,
and I'm thinking about how we never have to think
about what we were mixed up in.
About what our folks had to do with slavery.
Participation.
Even though our family was poor.
I always thought being poor
meant we didn't partake of America's curse.

Now *always* is such a long time
and doesn't make any sense in the corner of my mind I fenced off
that Sunday afternoon when Victor showed the picture
and everybody just talked about our relations.
Now that I've brought it up, could we talk.
Reconsider.
No, I mean right now.

Cultivation

When he wasn't crisscrossing the country
trying to persuade people to work together in peace,
Dad tended his garden in the evening after work.

He unfolded himself from the cigarette-stale carpool car,
gave us each a hug, and disappeared into the cellar
to put on tattered khakis and a faded shirt
that smelled of soil and sweat.

After loading his tools into the wheelbarrow,
he pushed it between a row of beans, corn, peas—
all the crops we'd need for the year—
with extra planted for passing rabbits and deer.
Wide, straight rows, carefully tended
except where gangly tomato vines
crawled over everything unrestrained.

Come July, the spidery blooms gave way to marble-size balls.
Green that brightened to yellow, orange, fiery red—
you never knew what color until the fruit began to blush.

Taking the wash off the line, I watched Dad stop,
lean one arm on the hoe handle,
pluck a handful of ripe cherry tomatoes,
and, using his marble-shooting thumb,
pop one after another in his mouth.
Slake his thirst. Enjoy what was free.

His refreshment seemed unsavory to me then
because those vines volunteered where Dad spread sludge
from the sewage plant just this side of the city he worked in.
Surviving seeds thrived in soil my father made
from hard, native clay mixed with human hair from a local barber,
manure from the remnant of our neighbor's farm
after his pasture turned into houses,
and night soil laced with prodigal nightshades.
Manna.

Appearances

We were walking along a stream where I wandered as a child
when Dad told me that as a boy alone in the woods
one day, an angel appeared
to say, *Fate, take your questions and doubt as signs.*
I knew Dad had often argued with his father
about predestination and the Bible's literal words.
So I thought I understood how the angel
countered his father's flinty dogma
and maybe the nickname *Fate,* which likely arose
from country folks' drawly way to deal with *Lafayette*
but also set a seal on a boy who wore a look of wonder.

As Dad grew old, he changed his mind,
deciding his Scripture-quoting sire liked to wrestle
with his son over salvation and the Word
because when his father wasn't serving customers,
he lifted a volume from the row of law books
behind the store counter, read a case,
and gazed beyond the shelves of neatly stacked dry goods
to weigh the arguments.

What brought my father's angel to mind that day,
in my time of inarticulate confusion?
Dad often spoke obliquely and was wary of being too sure.
What I was sure of was that, like Jacob's angel, Dad's visitor
had marked a tender place he chose to show me.
In a few months I would make my mulish husband go.
Though stones are slippery in a roiling stream,
I found I could cross by stepping from question to question.

Eve Celebrant

Encountering Marianna Pineda's "Eve Celebrant"
in deCordova Sculpture Park

As though she burst from earth's belly fully formed
Eve strides boldly across the hillside
raised foot making air a solid step
certainty in her clairvoyant gaze
No temptress
she offers two gestures of counsel
One hand tenders a pomegranate
jewel of possibility
She thrusts her other arm forward
hand upturned to say
Do not pass by before you consider
that you will know sweet juice and ruby-bitter seed
You too were wax
molded for beauty's sake
cast in strength
Miss all mystery if you impose a snake
Celebrate what you cannot predict

Changing My Mind

I get to feeling crazy at the end of a long day
when folks on the bus use their cellphones
to rattle on, fuss, and wrap me in their deals.

The prattle inside my head already sounds like
a phone call back in the days when conversations collided
on what was wryly known as a "party line."

But today in a nearby seat a baritone on Bluetooth
murmurs in om-like *hmms* between peaceful pauses
that close with a coda—*I love you.*

Da capo with variation: the bus motor hums
while my mind chants *love you, love you, love you,
love you* all the way home.

My First Mango, New Orleans French Quarter

After sipping frothy espresso and sampling sweet beignets,
we strolled through the outdoor market, senses feasting
on fragrant bay leaf boughs, flowers, and tropical fruits.

As soon as I beheld the mounded mangos,
the smiling vendor, divining my desire, chose one for me—
heavy, firm and yielding, with a rosy blush.

Back in our hotel room, you watched, grinning
as I peeled the fruit to reveal the gold, slick and shiny.
I licked juice from between my dripping fingers.

How your face rhymed my delight—
like when I first tasted you.

Dance Lessons

When the orchestra starts,
our teacher wiggles in her chair and jumps up.
She has injured a knee but cannot stay seated.
Step tap, step tap,

she sashays toward us, swiveling her shoulders,
extending an arm, palm up, enticing.
A flick of corkscrew curls, ginger and shiny.
Eyes aglow, sassy. Sinatra sings,

Just the way you look tonight.
We look tonight like aging women,
most perched on the edges of chairs,
tapping feet to the beat—as we are able.

This dance is new.
Her boys, as she calls two grown sons,
have visited and left,
emptying the house again. She cried.

One day, she found herself humming.
She jazzed around the living room
until her body conceived eight-count patterns
and bore them into spaces sadness had stilled.

She tells us so that when we *tap, tap, slide,*
we know the shadow side.
Delight takes the grim reaper for a spin.
I copy her, unspool my arms,

fingers outstretched to pluck the air
as though reaching for a ripe grape.
Our Ginger Rogers prances toward the camera,
inviting us to join her,

welcome whatever comes next.

Permissions

Opening epigraph: George Herbert, "Prayer" (public domain)

"Passagère" epigraph: Rainer Maria Rilke, *Poèmes en Langue Française,* Vergers no. 51. Originally published by Éditions Gallimard, 1926 (public domain)

"Living Room," "Room, Patterned in August" epigraphs: "House and Universe" from *The Poetics of Space* by Gaston Bachelard, translated by Maria Jolas, copyright 1958 by Presses Universitaires de France. Translation copyright 1964 by Penguin Random House LLC. Used by permission of Penguin Classics, an imprint of Penguin Publishing Group, a division of Penguin Random House LLC. All rights reserved.

"Relief" epigraph: Blaise Pascal (public domain)

"Bad Boys" epigraph: one line from *Soul Talk, Song Language,* copyright 2011 by Joy Harjo. Published by Wesleyan University Press. Used with permission.

About the Author

Although she grew up in the Washington, D. C. area, Merryn Rutledge's rural, southern roots show up throughout her work. Her poems have been published widely, and her book reviews have been featured in *Tupelo Quarterly, Pedestal,* and elsewhere. Writing poetry and reviewing new poem collections is Merryn's third career. After completing a Master's and BA with Honors in English from Smith College, Merryn taught literature and writing at Phillips Exeter Academy for many years. She then earned a doctorate in leadership and ran a leadership development and executive coaching firm. During this period, her essays based on field research on leadership were published in peer-reviewed journals, as books, and as book chapters. A transplant to Vermont and now eastern Massachusetts, she works for social justice causes, sings, dances, and enjoys the woods, marshes, and seashore. Merryn is at www.merrynpoetry.org.

Merryn is grateful for teachers Ellen Bass, Mark S. Burrows, Dorianne Laux, Miss Shockey (wherever you are), and for colleague-guides Nancy Cherico, Mary E. Cronin, Elizabeth Torrey, Brett Warren, and Joyce Wilson.

www.ingramcontent.com/pod-product-compliance
Lightning Source LLC
Chambersburg PA
CBHW031202160426
43193CB00008B/476